Celebrate Leadership

Lessons for Middle School Students

Maggie Meyer
Jenna Glock

Rowman & Littlefield Education
Lanham, Maryland • Toronto • Oxford
2006

Published in the United States of America
by Rowman & Littlefield Education
A Division of Rowman & Littlefield Publishers, Inc.
A wholly owned subsidary of The Rowman & Littlefield Publishing Group, Inc.
4501 Forbes Boulevard, Suite 200, Lanham, Maryland 20706
www.rowmaneducation.com

PO Box 317
Oxford
OX2 9RU, UK

British Library Cataloguing in Publication Information Available

Library of Congress Cataloging-in-Publication Data
Meyer, Maggie (Margaret) 1947–
  Celebrate leadership : lessons for middle school students / Maggie Meyer, Jenna Glock.
    p. cm.
  Includes bibliographical references.
  ISBN-13: 978-1-57886-303-7 (pbk. : alk. paper)
  ISBN-10: 1-57886-303-1
 1. Middle school education–Activity programs–United States. 2. Leadership–Study and
teaching–Activity programs–United States. I. Glock, Jenna, 1967– II. Title.
  LB1623.5.M49 2006
  373.1102–dc22   2005023118

♾™The paper used in this publication meets the minimum requirements of
American National Standard for Information Sciences—Permanence of
Paper for Printed Library Materials, ANSI/NISO Z39.48-1992.
Manufactured in the United States of America.

Contents

Foreword

Every teacher should be fortunate enough to have Maggie Meyer and Jenna Glock as teammates and collaborators. Every principal should be lucky enough to have them on his or her faculty. Since that's not feasible, *Celebrate Leadership* offers the next best possibility.

In this rich book, Maggie and Jenna provide creativity and inspiration, but that's just the beginning. They take an idea that is all too rare in education—that learning should be a celebration—and they show, step-by-step, how it can happen. The master teacher and novice will find bold ideas next to specific strategies and tips. Multiple intelligences strategies are offered next to websites and rubrics. This book offers a wealth of ideas on goal setting, student assessment, and parent communication, all within the framework of leadership. Studying leadership in this constructivist fashion means that students will not just become knowledgeable about leaders—they will learn to understand leadership.

Students in these kinds of classrooms learn the basic facts and skills that are needed to succeed. They will learn how to read, write, and calculate. In their discussions, they will learn more elusive issues; for example that Columbus really didn't discover America and that our environment is more fragile than it appears. Moreover, they will learn about motive, presentation, and collaboration. Through their work they will see events and issues through disparate eyes, they will learn how to persuade and convince, and they will learn how to be both strong leaders and good followers. Most important, students in these classrooms will learn how to learn.

This is true of those who use this book as well. Yes, it is possible to use the book as a recipe, following the directions in linear fashion and succeeding, and there is nothing wrong with that! Yet, knowing the type of people who will likely buy *Celebrate Leadership*, I expect that they will use its content and ideas as a reinforcement, as a stimulus, and as a provocation. Maggie and Jenna have done a great job of approaching complex teaching practices and curriculum designs. As a result, just like students who find success and want more, teachers who use this book will become more effective and find their work more satisfying.

The ideas and strategies that Maggie and Jenna present are timeless. They are always relevant in every classroom. That said, I believe that their voices are even more needed today in our high-stakes test environment. Thank you, Maggie and Jenna!

Tom Hoerr, Ph.D.
Head of School
New City School
St. Louis, MO

Acknowledgments

As educators we have moments when students and our peers provide us with purpose and inspiration.

To all our students: Thank you for sharing your gifts and talents with us. You have demonstrated that purposeful learning is not only a challenge but a cause for celebration.

To Gerry and Janet Sheehan, our curriculum pilot and tech support: Thank you for your problem-solving skills and patience despite the roadblocks we created for you . . . you helped and encouraged us to complete this project.

To John and Mary Pirie, our artists in residence: Thank you for being so willing to contribute your talents.

To Tom Hoerr, our mentor extraordinaire: Thank you for inspiring us to achieve more than we ever think possible. Your modeling and expertise are invaluable.

To our families: Your support for us as we leap into these professional projects is appreciated. Thanks for your understanding—and to answer your unending question of "Is it done yet?" Yes, this one is!

To our mothers: You were both incredible models for this topic. We are sorry we didn't get this completed in time so you could have held it in your hands. We loved hearing how proud you were of us.

Introduction

Enriching, rigorous, meaningful—these are the learning opportunities that are interwoven *Celebrate Leadership*. In our classrooms at various times, we find ourselves wondering if students are grasping the content. Do they really understand? In this publication the ideas of Howard Gardner have been our guides in designing curriculum and assessments that will engage learners. Constructing learning experiences that are based on the multiple intelligences and the standards provides all students with the opportunity to be successful. When it comes to assessment of that learning, educators can use the same concept in designing authentic situations. We call these assessments *celebrations of learning*. To demonstrate understanding, learners need to have options so they can show evidence of their learning through the intelligence of their choice. To be a useful assessment, that learning should be applied in a setting that demonstrates understanding. This book has step-by-step procedures, planning sheets for teachers, and all the necessary reproducibles that students need.

We have discovered that some of the most meaningful moments in teaching and learning have occurred during these celebrations. When students have multiple choices in ways to demonstrate their knowledge, the evidence of their learning is more accurate. We wanted the students to actually become the experts through the learning process. This assessment isn't just a fancy term for a presentation at the end of a unit. To actually engage in an authentic celebration is to witness a true display of student understanding.

The demonstration of true understanding should not be a score on a test but a display of learning that deserves a celebration. An ancient Chinese proverb states, "Tell me, I will forget . . . show me, I will remember . . . involve me, I will understand." Understanding concepts, not just learning facts, is what all teaching and learning should strive for.

This book is an integrated, authentic, standards-based approach to instruction and learning that allows for student choices and empowerment. The content of the book allows students to work on problems, projects, and products that genuinely engage them and motivate them to do well. It uses differentiated lessons designed around multiple intelligences that allow students to explore a subject area that will then lead them toward genuine understanding.

Following the introduction is a leadership overview that explains the purpose and rationale for the book. Lessons follow that will provide the support that is necessary for the facilitation and sequence of instruction. Black-line masters will be supplied for support of student-directed information gathering and time management. Traditional assessment is included in the form of scoring guides throughout the book.

The leadership project profile has the student self-assess and reflect on his or her own learning. Parents provide written feedback the evening of the performance. Included in the appendixes are the academic standards, learning strategies, and multiple intelligences that are emphasized in the book. Also, you will find a flexible timeline furnished for the teacher to help manage the flow and delivery of the instruction. After students have been engaged in the learning process, the teaching and learning culminates with a *celebration of learning* that is titled "Night of the Notables." The celebration has an authentic audience that may include peers, parents, and community members. We want this book to be a product that is easy for the instructor to implement, engaging, and at the same time worthwhile and rigorous for the students.

Leadership Overview

"What lies behind us, and not what lies in front of us, are small matters compared to what lies within us."
Ralph Waldo Emerson

"Ultimately, who you are is more important than what you know," states Tom Hoerr. This unit allows students opportunities to look closely at themselves, engaging their intrapersonal intelligence. There will also be situations that will provide them experiences to work with others and strengthen their interpersonal intelligence. (See Appendix B)

This leadership book provides students with information and experiences that will help them understand the characteristics of a good leader. Students research and define the qualities associated with good character attributes. The students choose from a project list and share the results of those assignments with the class. They then select someone from history that they consider to be a leader. To culminate the learning experience they later become that leader in an evening performance with parents and peers. A "Night of the Notables" will be the Celebration of Learning. Parents and peers try to guess the identity of the notable by asking just yes-and-no questions before the formal presentations occur. At the end of a two-minute expository presentation, the student reveals his identity to the audience.

By the end of the activities in this book, students should understand that powerful ideas and a good knowledge base need to be combined with interpersonal skills so leadership ability may emerge. As leaders we become more conscious of the relationships with others and become better thinkers and learners.

Academic Standards (See Appendix C)
Social Studies
Communication
Language Arts
Thinking Skills

Multiple Intelligences (See Appendix B)
Intrapersonal
Interpersonal
Verbal Linguistic

Internet Sites
Academy of Achievement Homepage
www.achievement.org

Biographical Dictionary/Biographies of Kids
http://garden of praise.com/leaders.htm

Men and Women of the World
http://homepage.oanet.com/jaywhy

Lesson Timeline (See Appendix A)

Other Resources (See Appendix D)

Leadership Lesson #1
Getting Started

Step 1. Read *Oh, the Places You'll Go!* by Dr. Seuss. What was the overall theme of this book? What was the author trying to say? Have a quick discussion about how this book relates to leadership. Have them brainstorm words that would describe a positive leader. Record that list on chart paper so it can be saved and used for following lessons.

Step 2. Present Essential Question: *What kind of a person do you want to be?* There are some positive characteristics and qualities that all people would like to attain.

Step 3. Compile a list of people that the students consider to be leaders. Record these on the board or on chart paper for future reference. Match up the names with qualities brainstormed in Step 1.

Step 4. Distribute student letter (1.1) and parent letter (1.2). Discuss the sequence and overview of this unit and content so when parents receive this information the student will be prepared to answer any questions.

Step 5. Assign Characteristics and Qualities of a Leader (1.3). The directions are on this handout. Explain that the words will be jigsawed and all shared in the next class session.

Step 6. Start to fill out and organize Student Time Management Calendar (1.4). Select and record a possible date for the "Night of the Notables" celebration. Fill in accomplishments for today and homework due next class meeting.

 Materials and Resources

1. *Oh, the Places You'll Go!* Dr. Seuss, ISBN 0-679-80527-3
2. Dictionaries
3. Chart paper/markers

 Pages to Copy

1. Student Letter (1.1)
2. Parent Letter (1.2)
3. Characteristics and Qualities of a Leader (1.3)
4. Student Time Management Calendar (1.4)

 **My Notes**

Dear Students,

Congratulations! You are going to become a famous leader of your choice. After we discuss the qualities and characteristics of positive leaders you will be involved in several assignments that deal with life skills and leadership attributes. Once everyone has gained an understanding of what a good leader is, we will research a notable person. One of the qualities of a notable person is that they have made a positive contribution that has withstood the test of time. You will eventually take on the persona of your research. On the evening of the "Night of the Notables" you will become that person and present your leadership qualities and historical information to an audience.

To accomplish this task you will need to follow these steps:

1. Organize a project calendar.
2. Complete vocabulary work that will help you with your research.
3. Understand how you set goals and make a plan to accomplish them.
4. Establish your own set of Life Rules.
5. Choose a positive eminent person to research.
6. Complete a Notable Mind Map Research Sheet.
7. Select three symbols for leadership qualities.
8. Assemble a costume that makes you appear to become your notable.
9. Plan a two-minute performance during which you will share with an audience the reasons why you are a notable person and leader.

Student Letter (1.1)

6

Dear Parents,

This leadership unit is designed to provide your child with experiences that will help him or her examine the qualities and characteristics of good leaders. We will be spending some time working hard to understand the terminology used to describe leaders. Some of the class activities will stress the importance of goal setting, listening skills and looking at other's points of view. We will be involved in selecting a leader to research and then we will end our unit of study with a "Night of the Notables" Celebration. Please mark *Tuesday, June 6, from 6PM to 8PM at the Mountain View Elementary School Cafeteria* on your calendar. The students will dress as their researched Notable and answer yes/no questions from parents and peers trying to guess their Notable's name. They will then share their research in a short presentation and reveal their identity to the audience. Please be supportive and share any ideas that you may have that will help make this a meaningful experience for them.

They have Student Time Management Calendars to work from. If you have questions about dates or assignments, your child should be able to clarify problems for you. If you are confused, ask them to speak to me about your concerns and I will do my best to help. If that doesn't work, the best way to contact me is through email at *mmeyer@nthurston.k12.wa.us.*

I'm looking forward to seeing you at the "Night of the Notables" Celebration!

Maggie Meyer,
Teacher

Parent Letter (1.2)

Characteristics and Qualities of a Leader

Research seven of the words from the list below. Write a definition for each word or phrase. Select someone you personally know and give an example of how they demonstrate this quality or characteristic. Give a different person each time you provide an example.

Example: Patience means being able to remain calm. My dad shows his patience when he smiles at me when I frustrate him.

1. Integrity

2. Respect

3. Patience

4. Flexibility

5. Courage

6. Empathy

7. Confidence

8. Positive risk taker

9. Good listener

10. Caring

11. Effort

12. Fair

13. Unique

14. Responsible

15. Perseverance

P.S. No one gets to choose patience because I have already done your work for you!!

Characteristics and Qualities of a Leader (1.3)

Student Time Management Calendar   Name:

	Date	Day's Actions	Homework	Plan
Lesson 1				
Lesson 2				
Lesson 3				
Lesson 4				
Lesson 5				

Time Management (1.4A)

Student Time Management Calendar   Name:

	Date	Day's Actions	Homework	Plan
Lesson 6				
Lesson 7				
Lesson 8				
Lesson 9				
Lesson 10				

Time Management (1.4B)

Leadership Lesson #2
Goal Setting

Step 1. Each student should have the opportunity to share with the class some of the seven words they worked on for homework. They should record on their handout the words others chose to do so their handout is complete and ready for future use. Take the opportunity for discussion where appropriate.

Step 2. Revisit *Oh, the Places You'll Go!* and introduce the concept of goal setting. To get where you want to go you have to have a plan. Just saying you are going to be a professional baseball player when you grow up is not going to make it happen. There are many different types of goals. Explain that for this lesson, students will work on a personal (lifestyle) goal. Some goals are longterm and others can be achieved in a short period of time. The students will have a week to work on a goal so it is necessary to help them choose a short-term goal. It is best to stay away from academic goals for this lesson. Present and discuss the student handout, Five Conditions for Effective Goal Setting (2.1). Walk through several examples of goals such as cleaning their room, doing their homework, feeding the dog, or possibly treating a sibling positively.

Step 3. Direct each student to decide on a short-term personal goal to work on this week and report back on next week (or class session). Since this is an activity from which all students should benefit, their choice should be benign and not too personal. Actually have them fill out the Goals and Strategies for Leadership (2.2) handout to engage their thinking and planning skills.

Step 4. Choose a few selections from the Achieving Dreams section of *Chicken Soup for the Kid's Soul* to read out loud to the class at the end of the session. Send them off inspired to accomplish their goals.

Step 5. The entire class should take out their Student Time Management (1.4) Calendar. As a teacher-directed activity, they should fill in the section that explains what they did as a group today, what their homework is, and their plan to accomplish their goal-oriented homework.

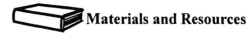**Materials and Resources**

1. Oh, the Places You'll Go! Dr. Seuss, ISBN 0-679-80527-3
2. Chicken Soup for the Kid's Soul, ISBN 1-55874-609-9

Pages to Copy

1. Goal Setting (2.1)
2. Goals and Strategies (2.2)

**My Notes**

Leadership Lesson #2: Goal Setting (2.0)

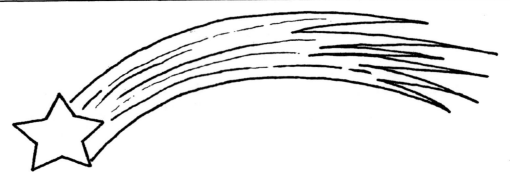

Five Conditions for Effective Goal Setting

Condition #1   **Goals need to be specific.**

"I am going to be somebody when I grow up." This statement is not specific enough. What does **be somebody** mean? *"I want to be a lawyer when I grow up."* Choosing the occupation of a lawyer can be planned for. It tells exactly what you plan to achieve.

Condition #2   **Goals need to be realistic and possible.**

"I am going to be the President by the time I am 21." This is not possible according to the Constitution. *"I am going to support a political candidate when I am 21."* This can really happen.

Condition #3   **Goals need to be controllable.**

"I am going to get my brother to like green beans." You have no control over your brother's taste buds and likes and dislikes. *"I am going to get my brother to try to taste new foods."* This is controllable through encouragement and creative planning.

Condition #4   **Goals need to be measurable.**

"I am going to get better at making my bed." This goal isn't complete enough. Data is needed. How are you going to measure this? What does a made bed look like? When are you going to do this? *"Twice a week I am going to pull the sheet, blanket, and bedspread up to the top of my bed and smooth them all out."* This can be achieved.

Condition #5   **Goals need to be simple in the beginning.**

"I am going to get all A's on my report card." This is a great idea but not a simple short-term goal. It requires lots of planning. *"I am going to spend one half hour on my math homework each night this week and check it to make sure it is accurate."* Don't make your first attempt at goal setting overwhelming.

Five Conditions of Effective Goal Setting (2.1)

Goals and Strategies for Leadership

All leaders can plan and accomplish goals. If you examine the backgrounds of eminent leaders you will see that they had the ability to set goals and attain them. For your homework you are going to set a short-term personal goal and report back to us on your progress. Select something that you really need to accomplish. Choose something that will knock the socks off your parents!!

Name_____

This is my specific goal. It is a realistic, controllable, measurable, and simple goal.
_____

These are four strategies and methods that I can use to attain my goal. This is my plan:

1._____

2._____

3._____

4._____

Goals and Strategies (2.2)

Leadership Lesson #3
Notable Research

Step 1. Each student will share the success of their goal-setting homework. The teacher will direct appropriate discussion when necessary.

Step 2. Review the Characteristics and Qualities of a Leader (1.3). These characteristics should be listed on chart paper and posted in the classroom if not already done previously.

Step 3. The teacher will facilitate the Natural Disaster Simulation. This team activity will reinforce and help the students analyze the aspects of the leadership role. Interesting follow up discussion should be a good assessment of student thinking for the classroom teacher.

Step 4. Write the term *eminent* on the overhead white board. Have one student look up the definition from a dictionary. The definition refers to people who are prominent and distinguished. In other words an eminent leader is a person whose leadership skills have stood the test of time and still are obvious even after their death. When students choose leaders to research, have them stay away from rock, movie, and sports stars of today.

Step 5. Distribute the Research on an Eminent Leader homework (3.2). Explain that they are to choose a leader off the classroom list that they compiled earlier. The person they choose should no longer be alive; they should choose someone they are truly interested in. This *may* be the foundation for their "Night of the Notables" presentation but they are not obligated to this research down the road if they wish to change their mind.

Step 6. Fill out the Student Time Management Calendar (1.4) to reflect on today and to help organize for responsibilities due next class session.

 **Materials and Resources**

1. Class generated list of characteristics and qualities of a leader
2. Natural Disaster Simulation (3.1)
3. Timeline Management Calendar

 Pages to Copy

1. Research Homework (3.2)

 **My Notes**

Leadership Lesson #3: Notable Research (3.0)

Natural Disaster Simulation

The purpose of this lesson is to give students the opportunity to apply and analyze their thinking about leadership characteristics to a simulation of a natural disaster.

Directions: Divide the class into small groups consisting of three to five students. Provide these situations in the following order:

Situation #1:
A natural disaster (earthquake, storm, tornado, flood) has hit the community. The entire school is forced into the gym for three days. Ask the groups to identify and list the three people who should become the leaders in this situation. Have them justify and explain a reason why they selected each person. Each team should report on their people and why they were selected. *Adults with proven leadership qualifications should be the end result here.*

Situation #2:
This natural disaster isolates the fourth (any) grade class from the rest of the school. They will be isolated for several days. No adults are present. Again ask the teams to identify (not necessarily by name) those who would become the leaders. What characteristics and qualities should these identified students possess? What behaviors will help the class get through this situation? Each team should report on their choices and their reasons for them.

Things to consider: Understanding the role of a leader in an emergency situation will differ occasionally from the role of a political leader or leadership challenges in other situations. Students should be directed to match the characteristics they are familiar with to people responding in a disaster. The teacher should help facilitate the second situation because the students will have more difficulty identifying a leader in this situation. Try to avoid having the students name personalities in the class.

Natural Disaster Simulation (3.1)

Research on a Eminent Leader

Record the full name of the person.

Where did they live?

When/where were they born?

When/where did they die?

What outstanding contributions did he/she make to history? Give some specific details.

　　　1.

　　　2.

　　　3.

　　　4.

Decide from your research three different leadership characteristics that your person demonstrated (use our classroom list and/or lesson #1 homework). Give a specific example from their life that demonstrates each quality.

Example:　　George Washington
　　　　　　　Integrity
　　　　　　　George couldn't tell a lie when he was asked who cut down the cherry tree.

Research on a Eminent Leader (3.2)

Leadership Lesson #4
Life Rules

Step 1. In groups of four, students should share their eminent leader research information. One student should be selected from each team to share their research with the entire class. Selection should be determined by criteria agreed upon by the group.

Step 2. The teacher facilitates the "Find the Leader" Game (4.1). This experience will reinforce interpersonal skills necessary for leaders to emerge and review the characteristics and qualities of a leader already presented in previous lessons.

Step 3. To further impress the value of emotional intelligence and interpersonal skills, have each team rate conditions and behaviors that are important when working together as a team. Have each team collaboratively fill out a Teamwork Rating Scale (4.3). The teacher can make an overhead and tally the placement (1-8) for each statement (a different color overhead pen for each team would be helpful). With that visual it is easy for the class to see which behaviors were considered the most important. Interesting discussion should follow.

Step 4. As a class, brainstorm a list of certain rules that a student should follow to make their life happy and successful. Keep this list on chart paper and hang it up in the classroom along with the characteristics and qualities of a leader and the list of eminent leaders.

Step 5. Distribute Life Rules (4.4). Explain that students should take into account all the experiences they have had so far in this unit when considering their rules. Take notes on the brainstormed list already constructed. Be prepared to share homework at the beginning of the next lesson. Fill out the Student Time Management Calendar (1.4).

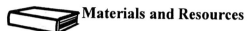 **Materials and Resources**

1. 18 by 24 inch white drawing paper
2. Find the Leader Game (4.1)
3. Packets of puzzles for the Find the Leader Game
4. Overhead for Teamwork Rating Scale (4.3)
5. Different colors of overhead pens
6. Student Time Management Calendar (1.4)

 Pages to Copy

1. Envelope Task Instructions (4.2)
2. Teamwork Rating Scale (4.3)
3. Life Rules (4.4)

 My Notes

Leadership Lesson #4: Life Rules (4.0)

Find the Leader Game

The purpose of this experience is to put students in a group situation where they begin to see the need for leadership behaviors. Before class, prepare a set of squares and an instruction sheet for each group of students. Numbers in the group can vary, but less than three or more than five makes the experience less effective.

Each team will receive five envelopes containing mixed-up pieces of five 6 x 6 inch squares. The squares are made of stiff paper and cut into patterns similar to those below. Several individual combinations will be possible but only one total combination will work. Cut each square into the parts. Label the pieces lightly with a pencil, A through O.

Mark the envelopes 1 through 5 and distribute the pieces like this: Envelope 1 has pieces I, H, and E; Envelope 2 has pieces A, C, and D; Envelope 3 has pieces B, G, and L; Envelope 4 has pieces K, M, and F; and Envelope 5 contains pieces J, N, and O. Erase the lightly penciled letters and instead write the envelope letters on the back side of the individual pieces so the game can be reused.

Divide the class into groups and provide each team with five envelopes and the instruction sheet (see next page) of your choice. Ask that the envelopes be opened only on a signal. When one team has accomplished the task allow them to be silent observers of the other teams.

Ideas for follow-up discussion:

1. What helped your team accomplish the task?
2. What hindered the task?
3. Did roles emerge for the members of the teams?
4. How did people individually contribute to the team's success?
5. What would you do differently the next time you worked with a team?
6. What would you do the same?

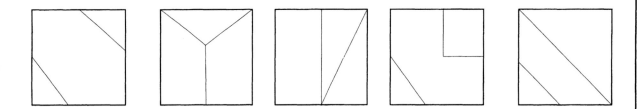

Find the Leader (4.1)

Envelope Task Instructions

Each team will be presented with five envelopes. Inside the envelopes are pieces that will form five squares that measure 6 x 6 inch. The task before you is to construct those squares cooperatively as a team. Each person should participate in the placing and positioning of the pieces. Everyone should be actively involved in the solution of this puzzle. When you have completed this task get your teacher's permission and silently observe the process that other teams are using to find a solution to the same puzzle. Be ready for a good discussion when all teams have finished.

Envelope Task Instructions (4.2)

Teamwork Rating Scale

Rate these conditions from most important to least important when working with a team to solve a problem. Number the section with an 8 if it is least important and a 1 if it is the most important. All others should be ranked 2-7. When completed, share with class to see how your team thinking compares the other teams.

Team members demonstrate respectful behavior to each other.	Team members demonstrate positive thinking and give each other encouragement.	Team members have patience and understanding for the other member's point of view.	Individuals in the team tolerate team member's errors and mistakes.
Team members are honest and direct with each other.	The entire team celebrates their successes and accomplishments.	Each member of the team is reliable and dependable.	Individual team members agree to what the team decides even though they may disagree.

Teamwork Rating Scale (4.3)

Life Rules

"We become what we do."

Chiang Kai-shek

1. Be honest
2. Always work hard
3. Never give up
4. Be kind to everyone
5. Be thrifty

What rules should you follow in your personal search for success? We will brainstorm a few ideas in class. Take some notes. Think over everyone's ideas. Think about what is important to you. Be a positive risk taker and choose your own life rules.

1.

2.

3.

4.

5.

6.

7.

Integrity means to firmly believe in principles that guide your life. What do you firmly believe? What do you care about? What kind of person do you want to be? Choose five rules that you try to live by every day. What are your rules for success? Make them general statements. Construct a poster. Decorate it. Illustrate it. Be ready to share at least one of your rules (principles) next week.

Life Rules (4.4)

Leadership Lesson #5
Getting Ready

Step 1. Read the provided paragraph about Helen Keller (5.1) to the students. Have them match information in the paragraph to the leadership characteristics on the classroom chart. What were her leadership qualities?

Step 2. In small groups, give the students the paragraph about Jackie Robinson (5.2). Have them discuss, list, and report on the characteristics and qualities he had that would classify him as a leader.

Step 3. It is time for them to select a person to research for the "Night of the Notables" presentation. Go over the events of the evening so they are aware of their expectations. Read through the Parent Letter (5.3) that goes home, and answer students' questions about procedures.

Step 4. Distribute the Leadership Mind Map (5.4) form to be used to gather and record information that they should include in their presentation. This is just one visual to help them understand the information-gathering process. They could use a note card for each category or you could design this step any way that works for you the facilitator. Sometimes the mind mapping doesn't allow enough space for certain information so improvising is necessary.

Step 5. Fill out and organize the Student Time Management Calendar (1.4) As a reference, use the Future Dates for Student Time Management Calendar (5.5) included in this lesson. Establish a due date for mind map research and to have students examine and record the other steps they will follow so they will have a successful evening presentation. Record the date for the "Night of the Notables" celebration on the calendar. Fill in accomplishments for today and homework due next class meeting.

**Materials and Resources**

1. Helen Keller (5.1)
2. Jackie Robinson (5.2)
3. Overhead of the original Student Time Management Calendar (1.4)
4. Future Dates for Student Time Management Calendar (5.5)

Pages to Copy

1. Jackie Robinson (5.2)
2. Parent Letter (5.3)
3. Leadership Mind Map (5.4)

**My Notes**

Helen Keller, 1880 – 1968

Helen Keller was born in Tuscumbia, Alabama, and deprived of her sight and hearing at the age of nineteen months because of a severe illness. She was also left mute by this situation. She lived in silence and darkness for five years until her parents found someone who could educate her. Anne Sullivan, who was twenty years old, and was partially cured of blindness, became her teacher. With Anne Sullivan's instruction, discipline, and dedication, Helen learned the gift of language in one month, learned to read Braille, learned to talk, and in 1904 graduated from Radcliffe College. Her education and training represent one of the most extraordinary accomplishments ever achieved in education for those with disabilities. Until her death at age eighty-eight she worked to help others by writing articles and books, speaking to groups, and raising two million dollars for the American Foundation for the Blind. Her greatest gift was her ability to inspire others.

Helen Keller (5.1)

Jackie Robinson, 1919 – 1972

Jackie Robinson was born in Cairo, Georgia, as John Roosevelt Robinson. He was the youngest of five children. His father abandoned the family five months after Jackie was born. His mother was determined to create a better life for her children so she moved them to Pasadena, California, when Jackie was a year old. As Jackie grew up he developed into a sensational athlete and was the first person to earn letters in football, basketball, baseball, and track at UCLA. In 1941, after college, he played professional football, but World War II ended that career. When the war was over he began playing baseball with the Monarchs of the Negro Baseball League. Branch Rickey of the Brooklyn Dodgers became aware of his talent and with his own act of courage invited Jackie to break the color barrier that existed in major league baseball. In spite of the pressure and the prejudice, he played well and was voted Rookie of the Year. It was his spectacular play that led to the Dodgers' first World Series Championship in 1955. He spoke publicly about injustice and prejudice. He retired from baseball in 1956. In later life he suffered quietly from diabetes and died from complications at the age of 53.

Jackie Robinson (5.2)

Dear Parents,

Your child is currently involved in a class project about leadership. It involves researching an eminent person and taking on that persona in a performance at the end of the trimester. The students will dress as their person, give a two-minute presentation of their life in character, and be prepared to answer questions posed to them by curious adults seeking to find out who they are.

You can assist your young actor for this presentation by monitoring their preparation, letting them practice their presentation for you, helping with costumes and supporting them with your attendance on *Thursday, November 21, at Mt. View Elementary, from 6:00PM – 7:45PM*. We are hoping that this early notice will help you mark this important date on your calendar.

The following is an overview of the evening:

6:00 PM	Notables answer simple questions from adults
6:15 PM	Adults guess identities
6:30 PM	Notable presentations and introductions
7:30 PM	Celebration of hard work!!

Please check off the bottom of this note and return it to me. We are looking for adults that will help us facilitate this celebration. We will notify you of the procedures if you have time to volunteer. Thanks for all your support!!!

Maggie Meyer

- -

I am looking forward to this night and celebration.

Parent/Guardian Signature _____
Name of child   _____

I am willing to help the teacher this evening by facilitating this learning celebration.

Phone or e-mail   _____

Questions:

Comments:

Parent Letter (5.3)

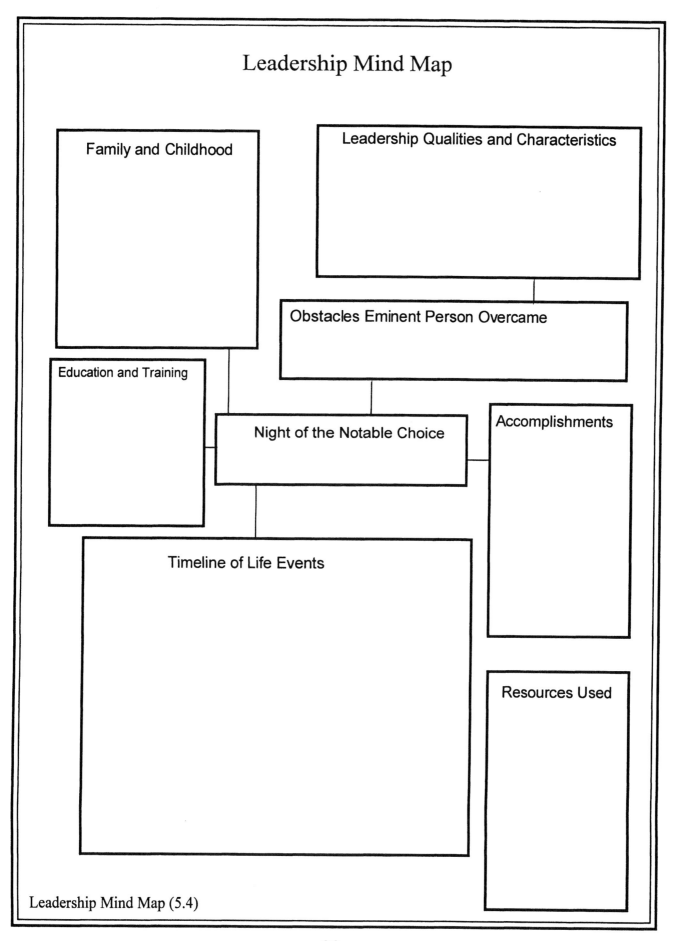

Leadership Mind Map

Family and Childhood

Leadership Qualities and Characteristics

Obstacles Eminent Person Overcame

Education and Training

Night of the Notable Choice

Accomplishments

Timeline of Life Events

Resources Used

Leadership Mind Map (5.4)

Future Dates for Student Time Management Calendar

Lesson 5 Date: <u>Day's actions:</u> Choose Notable for in-depth research	Lesson 6 Date: <u>Day's actions:</u> Invitations made in class and delivered	Lesson 7 Date: <u>Day's actions:</u> Mind Map due
Lesson 8 Date: <u>Day's actions:</u> Student-generated rubric for performance	Lesson 9 Date: <u>Day's actions:</u> Practice for Today's Evening Performance using class as the audience Peer score rubric	Lesson 10 Date: <u>Day's actions:</u> Reflection Day

Future Dates for Student Time Management Calendar (5.5)

Leadership Lesson #6
Preparing for an Audience

Step 1. Collect responses from the Parent Letter (5.3) sent home last lesson.

Step 2. Do a quick status check on student research. Where are you on the temperature gauge when it comes to your efforts? Are you hot, medium done, cool, or cold? Explain that at the end of today you will have a teacher conference with each of them so they should be prepared to ask your help or share some of their research with you.

Step 3. Review the Student Time Management Calendar (1.4). Today we are creating invitations, working on research, and talking about symbols. We will end the day with teacher conferences.

Step 4. Introduce the idea of symbols. Hold up a piece of gum. What leadership characteristic could a chewed piece of gum become a symbol for? Persistence would be a likely response. How are gum and persistence alike? Gum sticks to things. Leaders don't give up. Gum loses its flavor but you still keep chewing. Sometimes tasks get tedious but leaders don't abandon them. Go through the list of leadership characteristics and qualities posted in the room and try to match each with a symbol. Explain that during their presentation they will provide three symbols that will refer to the leadership characteristics of their selected notable. While completing their research they should keep this task in mind.

Step 5. If possible, purchase one invitation for each student. Having a manufactured invitation with an RSVP provides a formal flair to the evening. If that isn't possible give directions for the students to design their own invitation for family and friends. Be sure to include the date, time, place, and an RSVP for the student by a certain date.

Step 6. The teacher should conference with each student to get a handle on his or her individual progress doing research. During this time make sure each student understands that they need to have sufficient information for a two-minute presentation. The rest of the class can use this time to work on invitations and continue working on research while waiting to talk to the teacher.

Step 7. Fill out and organize the Student Time Management Calendar (1.4). Fill in today's accomplishments and homework due at our next class meeting. The Leadership Research Mind Map (5.4) is due next class session. Invitations should be distributed to family and friends at the end of this lesson.

 Materials and Resources

1. Posted list of leadership qualities and characteristics from Lesson #1
2. Purchased invitations and/or white construction paper
3. Student Time Management Calendar (1.4) Overhead

 **My Notes**

Leadership Lesson #6: Preparing for an Audience (6.0)

Leadership Lesson #7
Putting It All Together

Step 1. Read former President Bill Clinton's quote that was made to a middle school class. Discuss how that relates to being a leader.

Step 2. The Leadership Research Mind Map research should be complete. You don't have to assess or collect this work. During the teacher conference, students should have it for you to review and then you can address student/teacher concerns. Common concerns should be examined in a whole class discussion. Concerns could include: What if I don't have enough information? What if I have too much information? What are the expectations? Post on the wall or on an overhead the Project Review Checklist (7.3). Discuss the points on the checklist.

Step 3. Hand out Notable Performance Guidelines (7.2). Students should use this as a guide while practicing their presentation before the next class session. Use note cards for beginning, middle, and end of the presentation. Share with the students that an audience will usually remember the beginning and ending so make both unique. Have a parent or friend time your presentation. This would be a good time for the teacher to model a two-minute presentation. It should include how to incorporate the use of symbols for the leadership characteristics and the research from their mind map.

Step 4. Now is the time to introduce the concept of costume design. Stress that students should be able to put together an outfit to resemble their leader from within their closets at home. They first need to find a picture of their notable, and then they can get creative with it. A hat and other accessories plus makeup should add to the characterization. Students do not need to buy or rent costumes. They could, however, organize what they need, and then share that information with the class to see if anyone has an item they could borrow.

Step 5. Send Parent Letter (7.4) to the parents that volunteered to help during the performance.

Step 6. Fill out and organize the Student Time Management Calendar (1.4). Their homework is the organizing of their presentation into the beginning, middle, and end on note cards. They should practice and time their presentation so it fits into the two-minute time period. They need to find a picture of their notable and begin their costume design. Some students need to take home the parent letters that confirm the volunteered help at the celebration.

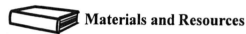 **Materials and Resources**

1. Note cards
2. Bill Clinton quote (7.1)
3. Student Time Management Calendar (1.4) overhead

 **Pages to Copy**

1. Notable Performance Guidelines (7.2)
2. Project Review Checklist (7.3)
3. Parent Letter (7.4)

 **My Notes**

Leadership Lesson #7: Putting It All Together (7.0)

"I can't live your lives for you. Every day you have to decide if you are going to be here on time with a good attitude, learning as much as you can. Every day you have to decide what you believe, what you care about, and what kind of person you are going to be."

-Former President Bill Clinton to middle school students
in Washington D.C.
Fall 1997

Bill Clinton Quote (7.1)

Notable Performance Guidelines

1. Have a very interesting beginning that hooks your audience. Use some music, read a quote, or show a picture. Make your presentation start differently than others. Remember that you don't give away your name until the end of your performance.

2. Speak slowly, loud, clear, and with expression.

3. Look your audience in the eye.

4. Stand up straight and don't fidget.

5. Have a beginning, middle, and end to your presentation.

Beginning:	Get your audience to pay attention to you. Be unique.
Middle:	This is the meat of your information. What life events have you chosen from your research? What are your Notable's qualities and characteristics? What symbols are you using for them?
End:	Give some encouragement or advice to the audience.

6. Include your three symbols and an unusual container to hold in your hand.
   1.
   2.
   3.

7. Include some character traits of your notable and give examples. Remember George Washington.

Trait	Example
Trait	Example

8. Reveal your identity and then offer encouragement or advice to the audience for the future.

9. Performance should last two minutes.

Notable Performance Guidelines (7.2)

Project Review Checklist

1. What are we doing?

2. Why?

3. When will this happen?

4. What do you need to do?

5. How can the teacher help you?

6. How does all of this relate to you?

7. Where do you look?

8. What does the teacher expect from you?

9. How do you decide what is important?

10. How does this relate to other things you know?

11. How will you share this project?

12. Who is your audience?

Project Review Checklist (7.3)

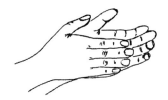

Dear Parents,

Thank you for volunteering to help us the evening of the "Night of the Notables," on *Nov. 21*. There are several jobs that need to be done during the course of the evening. We have highlighted the job with which we would like assistance. If you have any questions or concerns, please, email me at *mmeyer@nthurston.k12.wa.us*.

Greeter   These people will greet the students as they arrive at the front door. Each child will need a nametag and a number that represents their order in the performance. Also on the nametag is the room number where they will go to share Notable information. Direct them to the cafeteria for a walkabout and a short question-and-answer session. Nametags will be made ahead of time. All you have to do is check off the student's name on a class list when you present them with the tag. Obviously, you will need to arrive before the students. Any time close to 5:30 PM would be helpful.

Classroom Facilitator   You will be assigned the same classroom as your child's presentation. You will be responsible for setting up the room so the audience can have a good view of the Notable presentation. Please distribute Audience Feedback (9.3) form to other parents. At the end of the session collect these forms before parents return to the cafeteria. All students will have a tag with a number that tells their order for presenting. Please try to keep things flowing. You will have a class list to make sure that you know which student goes first, etc. Performances should be close to two minutes in length. We would love to have a picture of each child. Would you please use the disposable camera provided and become the photographer for the evening also. You might want to enlist some help from someone in the audience. All students should return to the cafeteria by 7:15 PM. Please supervise the room. We are guests. If furniture is moved, please return it to its original place. Give feedback forms and cameras to the teachers.

Parent Letter (7.4)

Leadership Lesson #8
We Are All in This Together

Step 1. Back-to-Back Drawing activity is a good entry point for today.

- Sit students back-to-back and give them each a piece of white drawing paper. Allow them ten minutes to draw a simple farm scene on white construction paper. They must include *at least* one barn, a tree, a fence, and a chicken. Stress they are not to peek at their partner's picture.
- At the end of ten minutes give one of them another piece of white construction paper the same size. He/she will become the artist.
- Allow one student to be the presenter and only he can talk. He must describe his scene and the artist will draw it. The artist may not ask any questions of the presenter but he/she can signal that they are ready to move on.
- After five minutes compare pictures. What kind of communicator was the presenter? How could they improve on the directions?
- Hand out one last piece of paper and have them reverse roles. Why are we doing this? (Improve presentation and communication skills.) Were you more successful the second time around. Why/why not?

Step 2. Ask each student individually what they are using for a costume. What do they need? Does anyone have anything at home that may help him or her out? Could they borrow it for the performance? Make sure every student gets this attention. Be ready to offer ideas and suggestions to help problem solve.

Step 3. As a class, generate a scoring guide for the two-minute performance. Use the board, overhead, or a piece of chart paper to display. A sample of a student-generated guide is provided. Have the final version prepared for the next lesson's practice.

Step 4. Allow time for the students to practice, while students and teacher conference individually to solve any last-minute issues. Ask for volunteers for the conference. Seek out the students you need to touch base with for support first. You may not have time to get to everyone.

Step 5. Fill out and organize the Student Time Management Calendar (1.4). Come prepared next week to present your two-minute performance to a peer for assessment using the scoring guide constructed today.

**Materials and Resources**

1. Two sheets of 8 ½ x 11 white construction paper for each student
2. Chart paper/markers
3. Sample Notable Performance Scoring Guide (8.1)
4. Blank Notable Performance Scoring Guide (8.2)

**My Notes**

Leadership Lesson #8: We Are All in This Together (8.0)

Sample Notable Performance Scoring Guide

Name/Notable _____

Peer Reviewer _____

	Possible Points	Awarded Points
Speaks slowly, clearly and with expression.		
Has good eye contact and posture.		
Speaks loud enough for entire audience to hear.		
Information and life events are presented in order. The presentation includes three symbols for important qualities that leader exhibited in his/her lifetime. The symbols are explained adequately.		
Conclusion includes encouragement or warning from Notable.		
Costume apparel is appropriate.		
Student has demonstrated obvious effort.		
Comments/Suggestions		
Total Points	100	

Sample Notable Performance Scoring Guide (8.1)

Notable Performance Scoring Guide

Name/Notable _____

Peer Reviewer _____

	Possible Points	Awarded Points
Comments/Suggestions		
Total Points	100	

Blank Notable Performance Scoring Guide (8.2)

Leadership Lesson #9
Practice Makes Perfect

Step 1. Students should come today ready to practice with their peers. For best results the teacher should pair up students who work well together. If time allows they may practice their performance a second time with a different partner. Remember to stress that the idea is to receive positive suggestions and comments on how to make last-minute changes. Provide each student with a copy of the agreed upon Student-Generated Scoring Guide (8.2).

Step 2. Explain procedures for the performance. A number will be placed on each student so audience members can match their guess to the number. The number is also the order of their performances. Explain that the audience will be giving students some valuable feedback and show them the forms the audience will receive. These will be collected at the end of the performance and shared with the students at the next session. Put the evening schedule on the overhead or the board so everyone is clear on procedures. Make sure they understand all the details so they can help their parents and friends understand what they are going to see and do.

Step 3. Share costume items brought for other class members. Are they marked with a name so they can easily be returned?

Step 4. Ask students for any last-minute questions, problems, or concerns.

Step 5. Practice as much as time allows.

Step 6. Practice, practice, practice.

 Materials and Resources

1. Overhead Copy of Evening Schedule (9.1)
2. Overhead Copy of Welcome to Night of the Notables (9.2)
3. Overhead Copy of Audience Feedback (9.3)

 Pages to Copy

1. Student-Generated Scoring Guide designed in Lesson #8 (8.2)
2. Evening Schedule (9.1)
3. Parent Handout: Welcome to Night of the Notables (9.2)
4. Audience Feedback (9.3)

 **My Notes**

Leadership Lesson #9: Practice Makes Perfect (9.0)

Welcome
Night of the Notables
Nov. 21, 2006
Mt. View Elementary

Presented by the students in the North Thurston Public Schools Enrichment Program

Evening Schedule

6:00 – 6:15   Promenade of Notables in the Cafeteria
Students are available to answer yes-and-no questions.

6:15 – 7:15   Presentations by Notables. Identities   revealed.

7:15 – 7:45   Celebration in Cafeteria

Sample Evening Schedule (9.1)

Welcome to the Night of the Notables

How many of the eminent people in this room can you identify? Record your guesses below and check for your accuracy during our final presentations. Students know a great deal about their notable person. Ask them questions that they can answer with a simple yes or no. We are trying to make your identification a challenge. Ask them questions that will make them think and reflect upon their life, their achievements, and the leadership qualities that made them famous leaders.

1.

2.

3.

4.

5.

6.

7.

8.

9.

10.

11.

12.

13.

14.

15.

16.

17.

Welcome to Night of the Notables (9.2)

Audience Feedback

Thank you so much for attending this remarkable evening of presentations by our famous leaders. We have brought together significant men and women from history to share their leadership qualities and characteristics with you. As you listen to their presentations please record some important feedback for them. At the end of the evening, give this sheet to the classroom facilitator, who will return it to the teacher to share with the students.

Presenter's Number	Something positive about this presentation was…	Something interesting in the presentation was…	A suggestion for improvement would be…
1			
2			
3			
4			
5			
6			
7			
8			

Audience Feedback (9.3)

Leadership Lesson #10
Reflections and Feedback

Step 1. Share the Audience Feedback (9.3) forms that the audience filled out during the presentations. Cut them up so that students only read their own.

Step 2. Have the students each fill out a Project Profile (10.1). Explain that this is great information for the teacher that will help improve this unit the next time it is taught. It will also be shared with the next group before they undertake this challenge. It should be very helpful to read about someone else's experience. Would it have helped you?

Step 3. Make up your own written assessment for the students if you feel it is necessary.

Step 4. Activities to choose from to culminate the unit as a class:
- Reread *Oh, the Places You'll Go!*
- Find another inspirational story from *Chicken Soup for the Kids' Soul*
- Play Twenty Questions
- Show digital pictures taken the day of the performance, if available

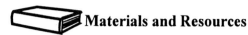**Materials and Resources**

1. Completed Audience Feedback forms (9.3) that were collected.

**Pages to Copy**

1. Project Profile (10.1)

**My Notes**

Leadership Lesson #10: Reflections and Feedback (10.0)

Project Reflection

Name_____

This is what I did.	
This is how I did it.	
This is how I feel about what I did.	
This is who helped me.	
A highlight for me during this project was…	
Next time I will…	
If I could have changed one thing it would have been…	
I learned…	
I think…	

Project Reflection (10.1)

Appendix A
Flexible Timeline

The Student Time Management Calendars presented on the following pages are samples of a suggested, flexible, management plan for instruction. Each lesson was designed to fit in a ninety-minute teaching block. The ninety-minute lesson block could be implemented once a week or as often as the teacher deems necessary. However, the authors suggest that students should be engaged in this type of learning for only a maximum of two lessons a week. Students need time to collect and then process information.

Student Time Management Calendar

Name: _____

	Date	Day's Actions	Homework	Plan
Lesson 1		1. Read and discuss, *Oh, the Places You'll Go!* 2. Brainstorm words that describe a positive leader. 3. Brainstorm a list of names of famous/notable leaders.	Characteristics and Qualities of a Leader (1.3).	
Lesson 2		1. Share homework (1.3). 2. Review *Oh, the Places You'll Go!* 3. Discuss the Five Conditions of Effective Goal Setting (2.1). 4. Plan a goal to work on for homework.	Goals and Strategies for Leadership (2.2).	
Lesson 3		1. Share Goals and Strategies for Leadership (2.2) results. 2. Natural Disaster Simulation (3.1). 3. Discuss term *eminent*. 4. Discuss research on a notable leader.	Research on a Eminent Leader (3.2).	
Lesson 4		1. In small groups, share homework, Research on a eminent Leader(3.2). 2. Find the Leader Game (4.1). 3. Teamwork Rating Scale (4.3). 4. Brainstorm Life Rules (4.4).	Life Rules (4.4).	
Lesson 5		1. Read/discuss Helen Keller (5.1). 2. In small groups, match Jackie Robinson (5.2) to leadership characteristics and qualities. 3. Distribute/discuss Parent Letter(5.3). 4. Discuss Mind Map (5.4). 5. Organize calendar (1.4).	1. Select a Notable person to research 2. Rough draft of Mind Map (5.4).	

Student Time Management Calendar

Name:

	Date	Day's Actions	Homework	Plan
Lesson 6		1. Discuss use of symbols in presentation. 2. Create invitations. 3. Conference with teacher on research efforts.	1. Mind Map (5.4) research needs to be complete. 2. Invitations need to be handed out. 3. Items that are symbols need to be collected for the presentation.	
Lesson 7		1. Discuss Bill Clinton's quote (7.1). 2. Discuss Project Review Checklist (7.3) to clarify issues. 3. Introduce costume ideas. 4. Parent Letter (7.4) goes out to parents that will help.	1. Using Notable Performance Guidelines (7.2) organize and practice performance. Use note cards to write out key words for beginning, middle, and end. 2. Find a picture of notable to create costume design.	
Lesson 8		1. Back-to-Back drawing. 2. Costume support sharing. 3. Students generate a Performance Scoring Guide (8.2). 4. Practice in pairs while teacher conferences with students.	1. Bring items selected as symbols. Put final touches on costume. Use the family for an audience. Have them time you. 2. Use note cards only when necessary 3. Organize costume materials to bring to class next session.	
Lesson 9		1. Use scoring guide, practice performance in front of peers for feedback before performance. 2. Go over celebration performance procedures. 3. Field questions and practice.	1. Practice. Use any available human being for an audience.	
Lesson 10		1. Share Audience Feedback (9.3) with each student. 2. Have each student complete a Project Reflection (10.1). 3. Ask each student to share the most important thing they learned from experience.		

Appendix B
Learning Strategies

Multiple Intelligences

The use of the multiple intelligences has been thoughtfully considered in the design of each unit. Howard Gardner defines intelligence as the biological ability to solve problems and fashion products that are valued in a particular culture and a community. He has identified eight intelligences and explains that we all process all eight in varying degrees. This book centers on the Interpersonal and Intrapersonal Intelligences. However, learning opportunities within this book provide experiences that strengthen all intelligences. Each of the eight intelligences has met a specific list of criteria and is based on empirical data.

- Linguistic: the ability to recognize and compose meaning in words.
- Logical mathematical: learning through numbers, order, and reasoning.
- Visual spatial: the ability to create visual images and transform them.
- Musical: the ability to learn, create, and communicate through rhythm, rhymes, and patterns.
- Bodily kinesthetic: learning by using the body in highly differentiated and skilled ways (becoming).
- Naturalist: the ability to understand the patterns, relationships and connections in nature.
- Interpersonal: the ability to work with and understand others.
- Intrapersonal: the intelligence of self-knowledge.

Understanding and using the theory of multiple intelligences will help teachers provide experiences for the instruction and assessment of students. According to Gardner, assessment should occur in the context of students working on problems, projects, or products that genuinely engage them, that hold their interest and motivate them to do well.

Providing for the multiple intelligences in instruction and assessment will determine true understanding. Understanding is the capacity to apply knowledge, facts, concepts, and skills in new situations outside of school and where they are appropriate.

The overall emphasis on the personal intelligences is evident in the individual research that is eventually jigsawed and shared with the entire class. The formation of work calendars and time management sheets help the students either work alone or possibly as members of pairs to accomplish tasks within an established timeframe.

Brain Compatible Learning

The lessons take into account the elements of brain-based learning by providing enriched integrated environments. The process outlined in the format of this book presents learning that is enhanced by challenge and free from threat. The authors have tried to keep topics relevant and related to real life. The learning culminates in a project, product, or a performance. The learning process is always stressed. The understanding of key goals and objectives is the desired end result. This is accomplished by exploring a topic in depth. Self-assessment through reflection is an important part of the evidence of learning and is encouraged in each unit.

Differentiation of Instruction

The authors use the term *differentiation* to mean the methods by which a teacher can manage a range of learners in a heterogeneous classroom. Carol Tomlinson, a national author on the topic, states, "A differentiated classroom is marked by the repeated rhythm of whole class preparation, review, and sharing, followed by the opportunity for individual or small group exploration, sense making, extension and production." Key concepts must be taught and the teacher needs to be very clear about what is expected. Teachers need to allow for choice and the freedom for students to make decisions on what to do with information they are accumulating. When students can differentiate the content, process, and the product, they are all motivated because they are learning on their terms and within their abilities.

Student-Directed Learning

For students to direct their own learning the teacher must provide freedom within a highly structured environment. A road map must be given, but the student can choose the route and design the evidence of their learning. The teacher should set and hold individual conferences with the student, which is vital for encouragement and problem solving. Materials, information, and resources need to be available for the students to pursue their interests at their instructional level. When students are involved in directing their own learning, it increases their motivation and develops lifelong learning skills.

Appendix C
Academic Standards

Essential academic learning guidelines are defined and outlined by most states. The units and lessons in this resource provide for these basic standards. Each unit focus overview will provide the teacher with the general standards covered in the unit. Listed below are the specific standards that you will see addressed in this curriculum.

	Student Standards
Reading	1. The students will expand comprehension by analyzing, interpreting, and synthesizing information. 2. The student will read a variety of reference materials. 3. Student will build vocabulary through reading.
Communication	1. The student will communicate ideas clearly and effectively. 2. Student will develop content and ideas. 3. The student will experiment with a variety of media and resources to convey a message or enhance an oral presentation.
Arts	1. Student will use art skills to express and communicate ideas.
Writing	1. The student writes clearly and effectively for different purposes. 2. The student writes with a style appropriate to the audience and purpose.
Mathematics	1. The student understands how mathematical ideas connect to other subject areas and real life.
Social Studies	1. The student will understand the characteristics and qualities of a leader. 2. The student will analyze historical information. 3. The student will locate, gather, and process information from a variety of resources.
Thinking Skills	1. Draw conclusions 2. Sequence 3. Brainstorming 4. Compare and contrast 5. Determine cause and effect

Appendix D
Selected Resources

Leadership

Craig, Susan and Kathleen Dent. *Take Five: 5 Traits of Competent Kids.* San Luis Obispo, CA: Dandy Lion Publications, 2001; ISBN 1-59363-153-7

Erlbach, Arlene. *Worth the Risk.* Minneapolis, MN: Free Spirit Publishing, 1999; ISBN 1-57542-051-1

Freeman, Sara. *Character Education: Teaching Values for Life.* Grand Rapids, MI: Instructional Fair, 1997; ISBN 1-56822-483-4

Karnes, Frances A. and Suzanne M. Bean. *Leadership for Students: A Practical Guide for Ages 8 – 18.* Waco, TX; Prufrock Press, 1995; ISBN 1-882664-12-4

Lewis, Barbara. *What Do You Stand For? A Kid's Guide to Building Character.* Minneapolis, MN: Free Spirit Publishing, 1998; ISBN 1-57542-029-5

Richardson, William B. and John B. Feldhusen. *Leadership Education: Developing Skills for Youth.* Unionville, NY: Royal Fireworks Press, 1996; ISBN 0- 89824-166-9

Roets, Louis. *Leadership: A Skills Training Program Ages 8-18.* Des Moines, IA: Leadership Publishers, 1997; ISBN 0-911943-52-8

Sisk, Dorothy. *Leadership: A Special Type of Giftedness.* Unionville, NY: Royal Fireworks Press, 1996; ISBN 0-89824-197-9

Ukens, Lorraine L. *Getting Together: Ice Breakers and Group Energizers.* San Francisco, CA: Jossey-Bass, 1997; ISBN 0-7879-0355-8

Ukens, Lorraine L. *Working Together: 55 Team Games.* San Francisco, CA: Jossey-Bass, 1997; ISBN 0-7879-0345-X

Curriculum

Hoerr, Thomas. *Becoming a Multiple Intelligence School.* Alexandria, VA: Association of Supervision and Curriculum, 2000; ISBN 0-87120-365-0

Gardner, Howard. *Multiple Intelligences:The Theory in Practice.* New York, NY: Basic Books, 1993; 0-465-01822-X

Tomlinson, Carol Ann. *The Differentiated Classroom.* Alexandria, VA: Association of Supervision and Curriculum, 1999; ISBN 0-87120-342-1

About the Authors

Jenna Glock has worked in a variety of capacities throughout her teaching career. For more than fifteen years, her educational experiences have spanned grade levels in the area of science, and she has worked with identified high-potential students at the elementary, middle, and secondary level. She currently works with middle level students in the North Thurston Public Schools system in Lacey, Washington. Jenna's background and training have been in biology, chemistry, educational technology, and, more recently, gifted education. Her passion lies in teaching and developing integrated curriculum that engages all learners in a variety of ways. Along with colleagues Maggie Meyer and Susan Wertz, Jenna has coauthored a book which focuses on developing the naturalist intelligence in students through the use of multiple intelligences and the science process skills: *Discovering the Naturalist Intelligence: Science in the Schoolyard* (Zephyr Press). Jenna is actively involved at the district and school level and serves on her school district's Math and Science Leadership and Students Improvement Plan Teams. She has also facilitated a variety of workshops and presentations in the areas of environmental education, multiple intelligences, the naturalist intelligence, and community problem solving.

Maggie Meyer has had many valuable years of experience as an educator. For thirty years her responsibilities were as an elementary classroom teacher. For the last six years she has worked with gifted and talented students in a variety of capacities. She is currently working in the School-Based Enrichment Program for the North Thurston Public Schools in Lacey, Washington. Along with Susan Wertz and Jenna Glock, Maggie developed a teacher resource book: *Discovering the Naturalist Intelligence: Science in the Schoolyard*, published by Zephyr Press. Maggie's other writing has been displayed in a variety of publications including *Educational Leadership* and *Clearing* magazine. She also has had the opportunity to be a workshop facilitator and online coach for colleges, including Harvard's Graduate School of Education. Maggie has extensive experience with multiple intelligences, community problem solving, watershed education, and developing gifted curriculum.

CPSIA information can be obtained at www.ICGtesting.com
Printed in the USA
LVOW101519310112

266397LV00005B/3/P

9 781578 863037